IT CAN'T BE DONE,
NELLIE BLY!

For the children of
Saratoga Independent School

Ω

Published by
PEACHTREE PUBLISHERS
1700 Chattahoochee Avenue
Atlanta, Georgia 30318-2112
www.peachtree-online.com

Text © 2003 by Nancy Butcher
Illustrations © 2003 by Jen Singh

First trade paperback edition published in 2014

Cover design by Loraine M. Joyner
Book design by Melanie McMahon Ives and Regina Dalton-Fischel

Printed in January 2014 by RR Donnelley, Shenzhen, Guangdong, China
10 9 8 7 6 5 (hardcover)
10 9 8 7 6 5 4 3 2 1 (trade paperback)

Library of Congress Cataloging-in-Publication Data

Butcher, Nancy.
 It can't be done, Nellie Bly : a reporter's race around the world / written by Nancy Butcher ; illustrated by Jen Singh.
   p. cm.
Summary: In 1888, a young, female reporter for New York World newspaper sets out to travel around the world in fewer than eighty days, while a Cosmopolitan magazine reporter tries to beat her to the goal.
 ISBN 978-1-56145-289-7 (hardcover)
 ISBN 978-1-56145-686-4 (trade paperback)
 1. Bly, Nellie, 1864-1922—Journeys—Juvenile literature. 2. Journalists—United States—Biography—Juvenile literature. [1. Bly, Nellie, 1864-1922. 2. Voyages and travels. 3. Journalism.] I. Singh,
Jen L., 1969- ill. II. Title.
 PN4784.C59B88 2003

                2003006306

IT CAN'T BE DONE,
NELLIE BLY!

A Reporter's Race
AROUND THE WORLD

by
Nancy
Butcher

Hoboken, NJ

London, England

Amiens, France

San Francisco, CA

North America

San Francisco Hoboken & New York

ATLANTIC OCEAN

PACIFIC OCEAN

South America

Yokohama, Japan

東

Canton, China

Singapore

Brindisi, Italy

Port Said, Egypt

Bay of Suez

Aden, Yemen

Colombo, Sri Lanka

Panang, Malaysia

London
Paris & Amiens
Brindisi
Port Said & Suez
Aden
Colombo
Panang
Singapore
Canton & Hong Kong
Yokohama

Europe
Asia
Africa
INDIAN OCEAN

Author's Note

This is a true story about Nellie Bly's adventures. I am grateful to Brooke Kroeger for her rich and informative book, Nellie Bly: Daredevil, Reporter, Feminist. Another great source is Nellie Bly's Around the World in 72 Days, which was her own account of her trip.

My book includes dialogue and thoughts attributed to Nellie Bly and others. Much of this was quoted directly from Kroeger's and Nellie Bly's books. In a few cases, however, I took the liberty of constructing dialogue or thoughts as accurately as possible from the existing record.

I want to thank my wonderful editor, Lisa Banim, for suggesting that I write a book about Nellie Bly. And as always, I want to thank my family, Jens and Christopher, for giving me the time and support to write.

Table of Contents

CHAPTER ONE

A "Wild and Visionary" Idea

Back in the year 1888, there were several big newspapers in New York City. One of them was called *The New York World*.

A reporter named Nellie Bly worked for *The New York World*. But she was no ordinary reporter.

For one thing, Nellie Bly was young. She was just twenty-four years old.

For another thing, she was a woman. In those days, very few women wrote for newspapers. The ones who did usually wrote about "ladylike" subjects such as tea parties and charity balls.

Instead, Nellie Bly wrote about the social problems of her time. These social problems had nothing to do with parties and balls. She wrote about factory workers who were treated badly at their jobs. She wrote about poor people who didn't have heat in their apartment buildings on cold winter days. She wrote about crooked politicians who took illegal bribes.

If Nellie Bly felt that a story should be told, nothing kept her from telling it. She didn't mind risking her safety or even her life to research and write that story.

Of course, not everyone was happy with Nellie Bly.

"A woman shouldn't be writing about such things!" some said.

"She should be stopped!" said others.

But Nellie Bly was unstoppable. She was fearless and stubborn. If someone told her, "It can't be done, Nellie Bly," she went right ahead and did it anyway.

One day, Nellie Bly came up with a story idea that went beyond anything she had ever written. Even she described it as "too wild and visionary."

Fifteen years earlier, a French science fiction writer named Jules Verne had published a novel called *Around The World in Eighty Days*. In it, an adventurous man named Phileas Fogg travels around the world in eighty days.

Today, with super-fast airplanes like the Concorde jet, a person can get from New York City to Paris, France in just a few hours. So the idea of going all the way around the world in eighty days may seem like no big deal.

But back then, there were no airplanes. People usually got around by trains, horse-drawn carriages, and wagons. Traveling twenty-two thousand miles in eighty days sounded impossible to most people.

By 1888, no real person had come close to matching Phileas Fogg's pretend record in *Around The World in Eighty Days*. That gave Nellie Bly her "wild and visionary" idea.

She studied dozens of ship routes and schedules. She considered the new railroad that stretched all the way across North America, from California to New Jersey.

She decided that Phileas Fogg's record could be beaten. And that she was just the person to do it!

Nellie Bly talked to the editors in charge of *The World*. She asked them if they would let her go on this dangerous and difficult journey. She said that she could write articles about it along the way and send them back to *The World* to be published. She told them that readers were sure to be interested in her journey. And she reminded them that more readers would mean more newspaper sales for *The World*.

As it turned out, the editors of *The World* had already discussed the idea of sending a real person to try to beat Phileas Fogg's record. But they wanted to send a male reporter, not a female one. They insisted that a woman could not travel alone without a man to protect her. A woman would also require too many suitcases for all her clothes. This was sure to slow her down.

"No one but a man can do this," one of the editors said.

"Very well," Nellie Bly replied in a huffy voice. She told them to go ahead and send a male reporter on the trip. "I'll start the same day for some other newspaper and beat him," she said.

The editors didn't want her to do that. They discussed and debated the matter. After a while, they promised Nellie Bly that if they ever decided to send someone around the world, they would send her.

Time passed. Nellie Bly worked on other assignments. But the idea of the trip never left her thoughts.

A year later, on November 11, 1889, the editors finally decided to send a reporter around the world. They kept their promise to Nellie Bly. They told her that she could be that reporter, if she still wanted to do it.

She said yes.

There was one catch. Could she leave by November 14?

Nellie Bly said yes again.

Now all she had to do was get ready for an almost three-month-long trip in just three days!

Most people would probably panic if they had only three days to get ready for a trip around the world. So much packing to do! So many details to arrange!

But Nellie Bly did what she always did. She went into action.

On Tuesday morning at ten o'clock sharp, she went to see a dressmaker named William Ghormley. She ordered one traveling gown that she could wear for most of the trip. She told Mr. Ghormley that she needed it in twelve hours.

By Wednesday morning, the gown was done. The cloth was woven in a blue plaid pattern. It was made of a strong kind of fabric called broadcloth.

Another dressmaker, Florence Wheelwright, made Nellie Bly a lighter gown that would be better for warm weather. She, too, finished the gown in a day.

At *The World*, Nellie Bly's co-workers were busy helping her get ready for the trip. She didn't have a passport, and she needed one to travel to other countries. So the newspaper sent someone to Washington, D.C., to get her a temporary passport. James G. Blaine, the Secretary of State who worked under President

Harrison, made up a passport for Nellie Bly overnight. Normally, she would have had to wait weeks, maybe even months, to get a passport.

Nellie Bly was eager to visit Jules Verne, the author of *Around The World in Eighty Days*. Monsieur Verne lived with his wife in France. So another co-worker at *The World* wrote to him, trying to arrange a visit. Hopefully, Monsieur Verne would be just as eager to meet Nellie Bly, since she wanted to beat the record of his character, Phileas Fogg.

The editors at *The World* had been afraid of sending Nellie Bly because they thought that ladies needed a lot of trunks and suitcases to travel. But Nellie Bly packed only one small bag. It was seven inches tall and sixteen inches wide—about the size of a big loaf of bread.

Because the bag was so small, Nellie Bly couldn't take the warm-weather gown that Florence Wheelwright had made for her. She only had room for a blazer, some underwear, several caps and veils, a dressing gown, a pair of slippers, writing supplies, and a few other items.

Nellie Bly's small bag did not include a gun. Some people had warned her that she should pack one for protection. But she had decided not to. She felt sure that the people she would meet on her trip would welcome her

with open arms. And if she did need protection, she figured she would take of herself somehow.

By the morning of November 14, Nellie Bly was ready to go.

It was a bright, beautiful day. Nellie Bly arrived at the Hoboken Pier to board the steamship *Augusta Victoria*. The ship was bound for England. Nellie Bly had her small bag with her, packed to the brim. She also brought a raincoat and an overcoat. She wore the William Ghormley dress, which would be her only dress for the entire trip. She also wore a special ring on her thumb. She called it her "lucky thumb ring."

Nellie Bly kept her money in two places: in her pocket and in a tiny bag that was tied around her neck. She carried 200 English pounds, which was the kind of money she would need in England. She took some American money, too.

She also wore two watches. One of them would be set on New York time for the whole trip. She planned to reset the other one with each new time zone she crossed. England was six hours ahead of New York, for example. So if her New York watch said 2 P.M. when the ship arrived in England, she would have to reset the other watch for 8 P.M.

She had bought a ticket to use as far as London,

England. But that was it. She would have to get the rest of her tickets in London and other places along the way.

Some of Nellie Bly's friends came to the pier to see her off on her journey. "Keep up your courage," they told her.

The whistle blew. Nellie Bly waved her good-byes. Minutes later, the *Augusta Victoria* glided into the bay.

And so Nellie Bly set off for her trip around the world. She stood on the deck and watched her friends on the pier grow farther and farther away. She wondered about the terrible things she might run into on her travels. There might be storms, shipwrecks, diseases, or even worse.

The twenty-five-year-old reporter was usually very brave. But as the ship sailed away, she experienced a rare moment of fear. She was not only leaving the shores of her home. She was also leaving behind her family, her friends, her work. She had no idea what she would face over the next few months.

"I am off," she said to herself. "And shall I ever get back?"

CHAPTER TWO

Aboard the *Augusta Victoria*

As the *Augusta Victoria* sailed away from shore, Nellie Bly stopped thinking about the long journey ahead of her. She started thinking about something more urgent.

What if she got seasick?

Nellie Bly had never been on a sea voyage before. She had no idea if she would come down with what some people called "the disease of the wave." Seasickness could be terrible, she had heard. The rolling motion of a boat could make a person violently ill. Again and again. Day after day.

As if reading her mind, someone on the ship asked her: "Do you get seasick?" Just *hearing* the word "seasick" made Nellie Bly feel queasy inside. She ran to the railing of the ship, leaned over, and threw up.

A lot of people were watching her with smiles and sneers on their faces. "And she's going around the world!" one man teased.

Everyone laughed. Nellie Bly laughed, too. She didn't care that all these people doubted her. She knew that she *would* make it around the world. Even if she threw up the entire way.

That night at dinner, Nellie Bly sat at a table with the ship's captain. His name was Captain Albers. It was a fun, lively dinner with lots of conversation.

Nellie Bly tried to eat the soup and fish and the rest of the delicious meal. But she ended up having to leave the table three times to throw up some more. When she came back to the table the third time, the other passengers cheered: "Bravo!" People were beginning to realize that Nellie Bly was unstoppable.

Nellie Bly almost got sick a fourth time. But instead she bravely told everyone that the dinner had been very good. Then she excused herself and went to bed early.

Nellie Bly slept and slept and slept. She had terrible dreams. Maybe because it was her first day at sea. Or maybe because she had been so sick.

She was awakened by a cheerful voice. It was Captain Albers. A few other people from the ship were with him.

"We were afraid that you were dead," the captain said.

"I always sleep late in the morning," Nellie Bly answered.

The captain laughed. He told her it was way past morning. It was four-thirty in the afternoon!

Nellie Bly had slept for almost an entire day. But the sleep had done her good. She got up and ate every single course of her dinner—without throwing up!

For the next few days of the journey, the weather was stormy. The *Augusta Victoria* made her way through high winds and choppy waves. But Nellie Bly was happy. Her seasickness seemed to have disappeared. And she enjoyed watching and listening to the other people on the ship.

Some of the passengers had strange ways of keeping themselves busy on the long trip. There was a man who counted every one of his steps whenever he walked. There was another man who took his pulse all day.

One woman had not changed her clothes since the ship left New York. "I am sure we are all going down," the woman told Nellie Bly. "And I am determined to go down dressed!" The woman was confident that the *Augusta Victoria* would sink. And when it did, she did not want to be caught in her sleeping gown or underwear!

Nellie Bly also got to know a family who was moving from New York to Paris. They had their pet dog on board with them. The dog's name was Home, Sweet Home. Its nickname was Homie.

Unfortunately, the ship's rules said that Homie could not be on deck. So he had to stay below deck with the butcher. The butcher was in charge of the meat for the ship's meals. The passengers worried that the butcher might not be taking care of Homie properly. In fact, whenever hamburger or sausage was served for a meal, some of the passengers whispered, "Has anyone seen Homie today?" It was a terrible joke that suggested that maybe the butcher had turned Homie into hamburger or sausage. But it was only a joke. Homie was fine!

On November 21, someone on the ship spotted land in the distance. The shore was still very far away. But everyone left the tables and rushed to the deck excitedly. Nellie Bly thought that they were all acting as if they were the explorer Columbus and his crew discovering America. Of course, she felt just as thrilled as everyone else!

At two-thirty in the morning, the ship finally reached the English shore. Their port was the city of Southampton. Southampton was about seventy miles west of London. Nellie Bly got off the ship so she could continue on to London. Most of her fellow passengers stayed on the *Augusta Victoria*. They were not planning to race around the world like Nellie Bly.

A tugboat took Nellie Bly and a few other people to shore. On the tugboat was a man named Tracey Greaves. Greaves was a reporter for *The World*'s branch office in London. He had been sent to meet Nellie Bly.

Greaves had some news for her. Some of it was good. Some of it was bad. The good news was that Jules Verne had agreed to meet her in his hometown of Amiens, France. Nellie Bly was thrilled!

The bad news was, there was no way she would have time to visit the Vernes *and* break Phileas Fogg's record. Amiens would take Nellie Bly off course by 180 miles.

But Greaves thought there might be a way for her to save time. "If you were willing to go without sleep and rest for two nights, I think it can be done," he told Nellie Bly. She agreed right away.

Unfortunately, there was a slight problem with that plan, too. They were already behind schedule. The last train for London had already left. And Nellie Bly *had* to get to London right away. Otherwise, she would miss more train and boat connections and fall even further behind.

But luck was with Nellie Bly. Somehow Tracey Greaves managed to arrange a ride on a special train just for the two of them. The London and Southwestern Railway had a mail train that was due to leave for London immediately. It usually carried only mail. But the company agreed to attach a passenger car so that Tracey Greaves and Nellie Bly could reach London by daylight.

Nellie Bly traveled to London in a small, uncomfortable train compartment. It had a single dingy lamp and an iron foot-warmer to keep her warm. When it came time to eat, she had to spread a newspaper across her lap for a tablecloth.

But Nellie Bly didn't care. So what if she wasn't traveling first-class? She was perfectly happy. She was on her way to beating Phileas Fogg's record!

Nellie Bly could spend only a few short hours in London before she had to take a boat to France. So she made good use of her time.

First she went to the London office of *The World* to pick up some messages that were waiting for her. She traveled to the office in a horse-drawn cab. Along the way, blurry images flashed by her eyes: Westminster Abbey, the Houses of Parliament, and the Thames River. But she would have to enjoy the tourist sights another time.

Next Nellie Bly headed to the American Legation to get another passport. The American Legation was a special office that helped Americans who happened to be in England. Secretary of State Blaine had gotten Nellie Bly a special passport before she left on her journey. But it was only temporary. She had to get a new one before she could travel to other countries.

The Secretary of the Legation, Mr. McCormick, started to fill out a passport for Nellie Bly. He asked for her name, address, and other information. He then asked her how old she was. Nellie Bly replied that her birth date was May 5, 1867.

That was not true. Nellie Bly's real birth date was May 5, 1864. She was twenty-five years old, not twenty-two.

She never explained her reason for giving the wrong age. Perhaps, like many women of her day, she worried that being a few years older would make her seem less attractive. Or maybe she thought readers would be even more impressed by her race around the world if she were younger.

Nellie Bly finally got her passport, with the wrong birth date on it. She hurried to her next errand. A cab took her to the office of the Peninsular and Oriental Steamship Company. There she bought about half of the tickets she would need for the rest of her trip.

Finally Tracey Greaves whisked her away to the Charing Cross train station. By this time, Nellie Bly was starving because she had not had time to eat. She was exhausted from lack of sleep. And she also had a very bad headache.

But a quick meal of coffee, ham, and eggs revived her. She boarded the train that would take her to a boat headed for France.

Nellie Bly was looking forward to reaching France. There she would finally meet the man who had inspired her "wild and visionary" trip—Jules Verne himself!

CHAPTER THREE
A Visit with Jules Verne

Nellie Bly took a boat called the *Paris Express* from the shores of England to Boulogne, France. Tracey Greaves, the reporter from the London office of *The World*, continued to travel with her.

Another uncomfortable train from Boulogne took Nellie Bly and her companion to the town of Amiens. When they arrived at the Amiens station, Nellie Bly saw that Jules Verne and his wife were waiting for her.

For a moment, Nellie Bly worried about how she looked after days of hard travel. Was her face a mess? Was her hair all over the place?

But her worries soon vanished when she met the Vernes. The couple greeted Nellie Bly with enthusiasm and warmth. She felt as though they had all been friends forever.

Jules Verne had a full head of white hair and a bushy beard. He had bright black eyes and heavy white eyebrows. Madame Verne, his wife, was charming and beautiful. She had smooth white hair, big black eyes, and a friendly smile.

The Vernes had a reporter from Paris with them named R. H. Sherard. Monsieur Sherard was to be their translator. The Vernes spoke very little English, and Nellie Bly did not speak French.

In fact, the only French word Nellie Bly knew was *oui,* which means "yes." The only English word Madame Verne knew was *no.* When the two women rode together in the carriage on the way to the Vernes' house, all they could do was say *oui* and *no,* and smile at each other.

It was early evening as they drove through Amiens, a pretty town with a park, little shops, and lots of women pushing baby carriages.

Soon they arrived at the Vernes' house. It looked magnificent with its high stone wall and courtyard.

Inside, Nellie Bly, her hosts, and Tracey Greaves settled down in the large sitting room. A fire crackled in the fireplace. A fluffy white cat sat on Madame Verne's lap as they all talked.

Nellie Bly was familiar with Jules Verne's history.

Jules Verne had been interested in travel since he was a child. As a boy, he ran away from home to be a cabin boy on a merchant ship. But he was caught and sent back to his parents.

In the 1840s, he studied law in Paris. But he was much more interested in theater than law. He wrote a play that was published in 1850. He was also very interested in geology, engineering, and astronomy.

In 1863, Monsieur Verne published his first novel, called *Five Weeks in a Balloon*. In 1864, he published *A Journey to the Center of the Earth*. These novels were followed by *From the Earth to the Moon* in 1866, *Twenty Thousand Leagues Under the Sea* in 1870, *Around The World in Eighty Days* in 1873, and *Mysterious Island* in 1874.

Nellie Bly could probably tell from Monsieur Verne's books that he liked to travel. Speaking through the translator, she asked the author if he had ever been to America. Monsieur Verne replied that he had been there once. He had visited Niagara Falls. He said he wished he could go back again and see the entire country from New York to San Francisco. But his health wasn't strong enough for a long journey.

Nellie Bly then asked her host where he had gotten the idea for *Around The World in Eighty Days*. He said he had read an article in a French newspaper called *Le Siècle,* which means "The Century." In the article, the writer tried to guess the shortest time it would take a person to travel around the world. The writer used a lot of math equations to figure out his answer. He decided that such a trip might be done in eighty days.

Monsieur Verne told Nellie Bly that his own travels had helped him write the novel. He once owned a yacht, and he had sailed all over the world in it. So he knew a lot about foreign lands. He used those details in his novel.

Monsieur Verne then asked Nellie Bly about *her* trip around the world. What was her route?

Nellie Bly replied: "My line of travel is from New York to London, then Calais, Brindisi, Port Said, Ismailia, Suez, Aden, Colombo, Penang, Singapore, Hong Kong, Yokohama, San Francisco, New York." She didn't even have to look at a map. She knew her route by heart.

Mosieur Verne pointed out that his hero, Phileas Fogg, also made a stop in Bombay, India. Why didn't she stop there as well?

Nellie Bly told him that going to Bombay would take too much time. She couldn't afford extra stops if she was going to beat Mr. Fogg's record!

At that point in the visit, Nellie Bly looked at her watch—the one that was set on French time. She knew it was time to go. The trip to see the Vernes had meant a 180-mile detour. And there was only one train that could take her from Amiens to her next stop—Calais, France.

If she didn't get to Calais on schedule, she would miss her train connection from Calais to Brindisi, Italy. Then she would fall an entire week behind schedule. If that happened, she might as well give up on her entire trip!

Nellie Bly asked Monsieur Verne for one last thing before she left. She wanted to see his study. That was the French writer's personal office. In his study, Monsieur Verne had written all the books that had made him so famous.

Monsieur Verne agreed, and they all went upstairs. Nellie Bly was surprised by Monsieur Verne's study. It wasn't big and fancy, like the rest of the house. It was a very small room with only one window. The furniture was simple and modest.

On Monsieur Verne's desk was a tidy stack of white paper. It was a new novel he had been working on. He showed it to Nellie Bly. She admired his neat hand-writing and careful editing.

Monsieur Verne then showed Nellie Bly his library, which was connected to his study. The library had floor-to-ceiling bookcases. The shelves were filled with beautiful bound books. Nellie Bly thought that the books must be worth a fortune.

Looking at the books gave Monsieur Verne an idea. He took Nellie Bly out into the hall. There he pointed to a large map on the wall.

Monsieur Verne had traced Phileas Fogg's route around the world on it, in blue pencil. He got another pencil and traced Nellie Bly's route on the map. She was very pleased by Monsieur Verne's gesture.

After such a wonderful visit, Nellie Bly hated to leave. But time was passing quickly. Downstairs, the Vernes offered their guests a glass of wine and biscuits. Monsieur Verne said that he wanted to offer a toast to Nellie Bly's trip.

"If you do it in seventy-nine days, I shall applaud with both hands," Monsieur Verne told her in French.

Nellie Bly was actually intending to finish her trip in seventy-five days. She could tell that Monsieur Verne didn't think she could do it in such a short time.

But Nellie Bly knew she could succeed—as long as she made that train to Calais!

The group exchanged their final good-byes.

Monsieur Verne raised his glass to Nellie Bly and said, in English, "Good luck, Nellie Bly." Madame Verne kissed her on both cheeks. This was a great honor, since French women didn't often kiss people they did not know very well.

The Vernes followed Nellie Bly out into the court-yard, even though it was chilly outside. They continued waving to her, their white hair blowing in the wind, as the carriage hurried away.

CHAPTER FOUR

A Rival for Nellie Bly

Back in the United States, *The World* was getting a lot of attention about Nellie Bly's journey. The office received bags and bags of mail for her each day.

Many of the letters praised the daring young reporter. They told her how wonderful and brave she was to be going around the world by herself. Some offered her advice about her trip. There were even some letters from men asking Nellie Bly to marry them!

But *The World* also received some bad news. Nellie Bly had competition!

A new magazine called *Cosmopolitan* had found out about Nellie Bly's plans before she left. They assigned one of their own reporters, Elizabeth Bisland, to make a trip around the world, too. Elizabeth Bisland left on the same day Nellie Bly began her journey.

Instead of going eastward around the world, Elizabeth Bisland was going westward. Her exact route was still up in the air. But there was a chance that the two "Misses B" might run into each other in Hong Kong. Some people joked that they might have Christmas dinner together!

It was even possible that Elizabeth Bisland might beat Nellie. That would be a disaster for *The World*—and for Nellie Bly!

Cosmopolitan magazine still exists today. It is a popular magazine for women.

Back in Nellie Bly's time, *Cosmopolitan* was very different. It was a monthly magazine that covered stories and news of interest to the general reader. It had been around for only three years. But in that short time, it had made a name for itself as a "growing literary force." Some people considered *Cosmopolitan* to be more dignified than *The World*. Nellie Bly's newspaper was known mainly for its big, splashy headlines and dramatic stories.

The race between Elizabeth Bisland and Nellie Bly was also a race between *Cosmopolitan* and *The New York World*. The editors at *Cosmopolitan* were betting that their young woman reporter would win. But the editors at *The World* were counting on Nellie Bly!

In the meantime, Nellie Bly had no idea that she had competition on her journey. She was too busy rushing from train to boat to train. In fact, she was so busy that she barely had time to send her articles about her adventure back to *The World*, as she had promised. Her trip was proving to be even more of a whirlwind than she had expected!

After leaving the Vernes, Nellie Bly said good-bye to Tracey Greaves, who went back to England. And she *did* make the train from Amiens to Calais. She ended up having to wait two hours at the Calais station before she caught the 1:30 A.M. train to her next stop: Brindisi, Italy.

Nellie Bly had been eager to leave the Vernes on time because she didn't want to miss the 1:30 A.M. train. It only ran once a week. It was a mail train and not really a passenger train. But the train did have one car for passengers. The car was called a "Pullman Palace." It wasn't exactly a palace, but it did have room for twenty-two passengers to sit, eat, and sleep.

Nellie Bly was not happy in this railroad car. It was

small and crowded. The air was thick with smoke from all the men who were smoking cigars and pipes. The windows were so dirty that she could hardly see the scenery outside. The temperature was freezing cold.

A dining room car was eventually added to the train. But the other women passengers told Nellie Bly that it wasn't proper for them to eat with men in public. So Nellie Bly and the other women continued to eat in the dingy Pullman Palace.

The train sped through the French countryside, past snow-peaked mountains. Near the Italian border, the conductor asked Nellie Bly several times if she was really traveling with only one small bag. He was worried that custom officials at the border wouldn't believe her. They might hold the train in order to search for the rest of her bags. Nellie Bly was finally able to convince the conductor that her little bag was all she had.

The train continued into Italy. It finally arrived in the southern Italian seaport of Brindisi at 11 P.M. on November 24—two hours late.

Nellie Bly's schedule had been calculated down to the minute. Arriving two hours late could mean missing the boat from Brindisi to Ceylon!

Fortunately, the *Victoria* was still in the harbor. Nellie Bly rushed to the boat and checked in. She found her cabin, which she would share with another young woman.

Nellie Bly even had a few extra minutes to run to shore and go to the cable office. She was anxious to get a message to *The World* office. A guard from the boat went with her.

When the two of them reached the cable office, Nellie Bly rang and rang a loud bell. At first no one answered. Finally an operator appeared. Nellie Bly explained to him that she wanted to send a cable to New York City. The operator replied that he had no idea where New York City was or how to send a cable there.

There was more discussion. The operator brought out all sorts of books to figure out how to send the cable and how much it would cost. All this took so much time that Nellie Bly almost forgot about the *Victoria*.

She was "quite well enough though somewhat fatigued," she wrote in her cable to *The World*. She explained that the train trip had been "tedious and tiresome." She added that she expected to be in the heart of the Mediterranean Sea within hours.

A loud whistle blew in the distance. It was the *Victoria* announcing that it was leaving. Nellie Bly and the guard looked at each other in total panic. She was going to miss the boat! And the boat had her bag on it!

"Can you run?" the guard asked her.

Nellie Bly and the guard took off like lightning. They dashed down the dark streets of Calais "with a speed that would have startled a deer," according to her records. The only people around were night watchmen and a few other people who worked late. They all stared at Nellie Bly in her ankle-length dress as she and the guard raced through town.

They made it to the boat just in time. Nellie Bly was saved!

At this point, Nellie Bly probably needed a good night's sleep more than just about anything.

Unfortunately, she didn't get one.

After she boarded the *Victoria* again and found her cabin, she went to sleep in her bunk. A short time later, she woke up to the sound of sloshing water. Her clothes were soaking wet. How could that be?

She quickly realized that her porthole, the ship window, was open. Some men were scrubbing the decks just above her cabin. The water they were using had leaked in through the porthole!

Nellie Bly closed the porthole and went back to sleep. She was still soaking wet, but she didn't care. She needed to get some rest!

She slept and slept the next morning, even though the maid kept coming into the cabin and bothering her.

"Miss, will you have your tea now?" was the maid's first wake-up call.

"Miss, will you have your bath now?" was the second.

"Well, you are a lazy girl! You'll miss your bath and breakfast if you don't get up this instant," was the third.

Nellie Bly ignored the maid and kept sleeping. She *did* end up missing breakfast. But she managed to make it to lunch, which was called "tiffin" on such ships.

Overall, Nellie Bly was not pleased with her experience on the *Victoria*. She thought that many of the English passengers were very rude. The captain of the ship, who was also English, was rude as well.

She also found the food miserable. Tiffins and dinners consisted mostly of cold soup, leftover fish, cut-up bits of meat, and cold coffee.

But Nellie Bly had some pleasant experiences on the ship. She spent a lot of time on the sunny decks during the day. She watched the men play cricket and *quoits,* a game similar to horseshoes.

At night, there was singing and music. One of Nellie Bly's favorite activities was sitting on the deck and listening to the ship's sailors below. The men, called Lascars, were from the East Indies. Every night during dinner, the Lascars would play tom-tom drums and sing musical chants, which Nellie Bly loved.

Nellie Bly often found herself to be the center of attention. Some of the women from other countries asked her what it was like to be an American woman. They told Nellie Bly that American women seemed to be so happy and free, compared to themselves. They said that they wished they could be as daring as she was. These women must have been very impressed by the young Nellie Bly, who was traveling around the world all by herself!

The men on board also paid special attention to Nellie Bly. There was a rumor going around the ship that she was a rich American heiress. So she started getting marriage proposals—just like the ones that were flooding into *The World* office back in New York!

One man told Nellie Bly that he needed a wife who wouldn't expect a lot of money from his family. He explained that his older brother would be inheriting all of his family's fortune. He needed a wife who could give *him* money!

Another man told her that he had always wanted to find a wife who could travel without a lot of luggage.

Nellie Bly was a smart reporter who never missed a detail. She had noticed that this young man always wore very nice clothes. He also changed outfits several times a day.

She asked him how many trunks he had with him on this trip.

"Nineteen," he replied.

Nellie Bly probably couldn't wait to tell that funny story to her editors back home. They were the ones who thought that *women* traveled with too much luggage!

CHAPTER FIVE
The Nellie Bly Guessing Match

The editors at *The World* were beginning to worry. Part of their reason for sending Nellie Bly on a trip around the globe was to fill the paper with stories of her travels. Nellie Bly had agreed to send back regular articles by cable. That way *The World* readers could keep up with her adventures. And *The World* would sell a lot more newspapers.

But the cables from Nellie Bly didn't always arrive regularly. Sometimes her editors would receive many cables in one day. Sometimes they would receive nothing at all for a very long time.

When there were no cables from Nellie Bly, the editors had to fill up space in the newspaper. They would often do this by quoting all the wonderful things people had to say about Nellie Bly.

The World had to keep its readers interested in Nellie Bly even when there was no news from their star reporter. But how?

One day they came up with a brilliant idea. They would run a daily contest called "The Nellie Bly Guessing Match"!

Readers would be asked to guess how many days, hours, minutes, and seconds Nellie Bly's trip would take. Whoever guessed the closest time would be the winner. The grand prize would be a free trip to Europe.

The World began running the contest right away. It was a huge success. In fact, by December 2, more than 100,000 readers had sent back the guessing ballots. The editors were delighted. It was only three weeks into Nellie Bly's trip. There were many more weeks to go.

The "Nellie Bly Guessing Match" ran in the paper every day for two months, in December 1889 and January 1890. The game kept readers guessing. It also kept them buying lots and lots of copies of *The World*!

Far across the ocean, the *Victoria* reached Port Said in Egypt. Port Said was at the mouth of the Suez Canal.

The Suez Canal had been opened in 1869. The canal connected the Mediterranean Sea and the Red Sea. Ships from Europe no longer had to sail all the way around the southern tip of Africa to reach the Indian Ocean. The canal had shortened the distance between England and India by 6,000 miles!

The *Victoria* would eventually sail through the Suez Canal to Nellie Bly's next stop, Colombo, which was in the country of Sri Lanka. But first it anchored at Port Said to get more coal. The passengers were free to go ashore and wander around the town. They could go shopping, or do whatever else they wanted.

Many of Nellie Bly's fellow passengers armed themselves before they got off the ship. The men carried canes. The women carried parasols. They all wanted "to keep off the beggars," they explained to Nellie Bly. The people of Port Said were said to be very poor.

The passengers tried to get Nellie Bly to protect herself, too. But she refused to carry a parasol or other "weapon." She told the other travelers that "having a stick beats more ugliness into a person than it ever beats out." Nellie Bly believed that treating people with trust was better than treating them with suspicion.

Once on shore, the passengers went their different ways. Some of them went on burro rides that were offered by Arab boys. Nellie Bly wasn't all that interested in the burros. She had lived in Mexico for a while and had seen burros there. She was more interested in going to a "gambling house."

A gambling house was like a modern-day casino, where people go to play games and try to win money. Nellie Bly and several other passengers went to one of the gambling houses in Port Said and played at the roulette wheel. They bet a good deal of their English gold money on numbers and colors on the wheel.

But Nellie Bly did not manage to win money at the roulette wheel. In fact, the longer she stayed, the less money she had!

She wanted to save some money for shopping. So she walked away from the gambling house with what she had left. Then she bought herself a few small things at the shops. She picked out a sunhat to protect her from the hot Mediterranean sun. And to go with it, she bought herself a light scarf called a *pugaree*. It was the custom in that country to wind the *pugaree* around the hat.

After a while, Nellie Bly took a long walk around the streets of Port Said. She never forgot that she was a reporter. She was always eager to observe details of everyday life.

On her walk, she saw old houses with carved wooden fronts. She saw many poor people begging for money and food. She saw lines of camels carrying firewood.

Nellie Bly was particularly interested in the way the Egyptian women dressed. She noticed that they wore shapeless black clothes that covered their bodies. They also wore black veils that hid most of their faces and fell all the way to their knees. Men, on the other hand, wore outfits that showed their faces and much of their arms and legs.

It was the custom of the country and its religion for women to act modestly and to wear clothes that kept them hidden from view.

It is hard to imagine what the people of Port Said must have thought of a daring woman like Nellie Bly!

CHAPTER SIX

An Unexpected Delay

Nellie Bly made sure she got back to the *Victoria* on time. The ship set off again that night.

The next morning, she got up earlier than usual. She was anxious to see the great Suez Canal.

Once on deck, Nellie Bly saw that the ship was passing through what looked like "an enormous ditch." There were high, sandy banks on either side. The ship was moving very, very slowly. Going any faster might hurt the sandy banks.

The slowness of the ship made the air feel even hotter than it was. But Nellie Bly didn't complain. She just put on her new sunhat and watched the scenery.

She saw Arab men and women on the shore, working in the hot sun. Camels carried stone to the workers. The workers then used the stone to strengthen the sandy banks.

The *Victoria* eventually reached the Bay of Suez and anchored. While there, the ship was met by a number of small sailboats called *falukas*. In the dusky darkness, Nellie Bly thought the *falukas* looked like white moths flocking to a light.

The men on the *falukas* had things to sell to the passengers, so they got off and boarded the *Victoria*. They offered fruits, photographs, and seashells for sale. There were also jugglers among them who showed off their juggling skills.

After leaving Suez, the *Victoria* sailed through the Red Sea. Nellie Bly spent the long, hot days on deck, relaxing.

The nights were also hot. It was hard for the passengers to sleep in their stuffy cabins. In fact, the men started to sleep on deck, where it was cooler in the open air. Women were not allowed to do so, however. In fact, the captain made a rule that women couldn't even go on deck until 8 A.M.!

Even though it was hot, Nellie Bly enjoyed her days and nights on the Red Sea. She especially liked seeing the sights.

One of the sights that impressed her the most was a group of tall brown mountains called the "Twelve Apostles." In history, the Twelve Apostles were the twelve men whom Jesus Christ sent out into the world to spread his ideas and teachings.

The *Victoria* eventually reached the port of Aden. Today, Aden is in the southern part of the country of Yemen. The ship had a seven-hour layover there.

The ship's officers warned passengers not to go ashore because of the intense heat. The officers thought the women might faint or get sick in the heat.

But Nellie Bly was not to be stopped. She wanted to go ashore and observe the local scene so she could write about it for her readers back home.

Aden was a small town surrounded by craggy, barren mountains. To Nellie Bly, it seemed as if the town were nestled inside an extinct volcano. The buildings in Aden were made of adobe, which is a kind of heavy clay. The hot sun had bleached the adobe buildings white.

The main street of Aden was crowded. There were people everywhere, carrying water in goatskin bags. Camels carried cut stone.

Nellie Bly was very interested in how the men and women were dressed. The men wore sashes around their waists. The women wore a thin silk cloth draped around their bodies, with no sandals or shoes. They also wore a single feather in their black hair. The feathers were red, purple, green, and other bright colors. Both the men and women wore a lot of gold and silver jewelry. They had beads, bracelets, and rings on their fingers and toes.

The young reporter thought that the people of Aden had the most beautiful teeth she had ever seen. They cleaned and polished their teeth with sticks from trees. She made a point of buying one of those stick toothbrushes to take back with her to America.

At the end of the day, Nellie Bly returned safely to the *Victoria*. She felt just fine. She was glad she had gone to Aden and not listened to the officers' warnings about the heat!

On December 8, the *Victoria* arrived in Colombo. Colombo is the capital of what is now the country of Sri Lanka.

Nellie Bly loved Colombo. It was lush and green, with magnificent houses that looked to her like marble palaces. In the background of Colombo was a tall mountain called Adam's Peak.

In Colombo, Nellie Bly and the other passengers

stayed at the Grand Oriental Hotel. There, Nellie Bly sat in an easy chair, sipped the delicious native tea, and wrote about the scenery and activities around her. Local women came by to try to sell dainty handmade lace to the tourists. Men in high turbans offered beautiful gems for sale. The jewels were displayed in little velvet boxes. "There were deeply-dark emeralds, firelit diamonds, exquisite pearls, rubies like pure drops of blood, the lucky cat's eye with its moving line, and all set in beautiful shapes," Nellie Bly wrote in her notebook.

At tiffin, Nellie Bly enjoyed spicy curry and Bombay duck. Bombay duck was actually a kind of dried fish. Nellie Bly complained about how smelly the Bombay duck was, but she learned to eat it in spite of the unpleasant odor.

Nellie Bly went out to explore the streets of Colombo. There she saw people riding elephants. She also saw a jinricksha for the first time. A jinricksha was a kind of taxi for passengers. It was a two-wheeled wagon that a driver would pull behind him as he ran. Because of the heat, a jinricksha driver wore only a sash around his waist and a big sunhat shaped like a mushroom.

Nellie Bly found out that she would have more time than she expected to see the sights of Colombo.

Her next ship, the *Oriental*, was supposed to take her from Ceylon, which was near Colombo, to China.

The problem was that the *Oriental* could not leave until an old clunker of a ship called the *Nepaul* arrived. There were passengers on the *Nepaul* that needed to transfer to the *Oriental*. Nellie Bly's ship would have to wait for them.

She would be stuck in Colombo for five whole days!

"NELLIE BLY DELAYED," *The World* headline read on December 12. Nellie Bly had sent her editors a cable and told them the bad news.

The World editors were starting to get worried. Nellie Bly wouldn't be able to sail on the *Oriental* until December 13. The *Oriental* would take her to Singapore, and then Hong Kong.

In Hong Kong, she had to catch the steamship *Oceanic,* which was scheduled to depart for Japan and then San Francisco on December 28. Nellie Bly didn't have much extra time in her schedule. And with the *Cosmopolitan* reporter, Elizabeth Bisland, trying to beat

Phileas Fogg's record, too, Nellie Bly didn't have a single day, hour, or minute to waste.

Would Nellie Bly make it? Would she be able to make her trip around the world in seventy-five days—*and* beat Elizabeth Bisland?

CHAPTER SEVEN

Stuck Again

On her fifth day in Colombo, Nellie Bly was told that the Oriental would be ready to set sail at eight o'clock the next morning. Finally she would be able to continue on her journey!

The next morning at five o'clock, she woke up, packed, and made her way to the *Oriental*. She was one of the first ones on the boat.

"When will we sail?" she asked the boat's chief engineer.

"As soon as the *Nepaul* comes in," the man said. "She was to have been here at daybreak, but she hasn't been sighted yet. Waiting for the *Nepaul* has given us this five days' delay. She's a slow old boat."

"May she go to the bottom of the bay when she does get in!" Nellie Bly replied crossly. "The old tub!"

Nellie Bly was *not* happy about the fact that she had been stuck in Colombo for so long. But the *Oriental* had to wait for passengers from the *Nepaul*.

Finally the boat came in. Passengers got off the *Nepaul* and got on board the *Oriental*. The *Oriental* was ready to set sail at last. Nellie Bly breathed a sigh of relief.

Once the *Oriental* had set out to sea, Nellie Bly's bad mood began to disappear. Soon she was having a good time. She liked the captain and his crew, who were all polite and friendly. She liked the food, which was delicious. And her cabin was very comfortable.

After six days, the *Oriental* reached Penang, a town on an island off the west coast of Malaysia. Nellie Bly went ashore to do some sightseeing.

She visited a Chinese joss-house, which was a kind of temple. The joss-house had a fancy pink and white roof with dragons on it. The dragons' mouths were open, as if the dragons were trying to roar. Their tails curved up in the air, as if the dragons were trying to attack something with them.

At the temple, Nellie Bly visited with the priests. The priests were completely bald and wore gold silk robes. She drank tea with them out of tiny cups. They couldn't speak English, and she couldn't speak Chinese. So they all just smiled and nodded at each other.

After Penang, the *Oriental*'s next stop was Singapore. The ship arrived there on December 18, 1889. By this time, Nellie Bly had traveled 10,657 miles in just thirty-four days!

The *Oriental* was only supposed to stay in Singapore for a few hours before starting for Hong Kong. But Nellie Bly got some bad news. The *Oriental* was going to be delayed for twenty-four hours. It would not set sail for Hong Kong until the following evening.

Nellie Bly was furious. She was also very worried. Every little delay meant that she might not be able to break Phileas Fogg's record!

But for the moment, there was nothing she could do. The next morning, Nellie Bly decided to get off the boat. She hired a driver and went sight-seeing around Singapore.

She admired the houses in town, which were painted blue and white. She saw many Chinese women wearing bright, pretty gowns. Their babies wore big, shapeless outfits that looked like pillowcases.

Nellie Bly stopped at a barbershop and watched a Chinese barber cut a man's hair. The customer bent over low while the barber worked. First the barber shaved off almost all the man's hair. He left only a single long strand that hung down from the back of the man's head. The barber then braided the long strand into a pigtail. As a final touch, he attached a silk tassel to the end of it.

Later, Nellie Bly saw something that looked like a parade going down the street. It was a funeral procession. The Chinese men in the procession carried black and white satin flags. Musicians rode behind them on Malay ponies. The musicians played fifes, cymbals, tom-toms, and gongs. Next came people carrying Chinese lanterns and roast pigs on long poles. At the very end of the procession were more men with banners.

Nellie Bly counted forty pallbearers. Their job was to carry the dead person's casket. The casket rested on long poles that the men balanced on their shoulders. A beautiful scarlet-colored cloth with white dots covered the casket.

Nellie Bly knew that she was watching a funeral procession. But the mood of the procession did not seem sad. It was happy and lively, almost like a circus parade.

After she watched the funeral procession, Nellie Bly decided to visit a Hindu temple. But when she got there, the priests would not let her inside the stone walls of the temple. One of the priests explained that they could not allow her in because she was a woman.

Nellie Bly couldn't believe it. What difference did it make that she was a woman?

She asked him again to let her in.

"No, Señora, no mudder," the priest said. He shook his head.

Nellie Bly thought "mudder" meant "mother." "I am *not* a mother!" she cried out.

But the priest refused to listen to her arguments. No matter what she said, he would not allow her to come into the temple.

Nellie Bly finally gave up and headed back to the *Oriental*. The *Oriental* was due to set sail for Hong Kong that evening.

On the way back to the boat, Nellie Bly's driver wanted to stop at his house for a few minutes. While they were there, Nellie Bly met the driver's wife and their children.

Nellie Bly also met their pet monkey. The monkey was sitting in the doorway of their house.

Nellie Bly suddenly felt that she had to have the monkey for herself. He could be her traveling companion for the rest of the trip.

She offered the driver and his wife money for the little animal. They agreed.

"Will the monkey bite?" Nellie Bly asked the driver.

"Monkey no bite," he replied.

Nellie Bly hoped he was telling the truth!

She and her new pet monkey said good-bye to the driver's wife and children. The driver took the two of them back to the *Oriental*. The boat was due to leave for Hong Kong in a very short time.

Nellie Bly was excited. Once she landed in Hong Kong, she would be halfway through her trip around the world.

What Nellie Bly didn't know was that she, her new monkey, and everyone else on the *Oriental* would soon find themselves in terrible danger.

CHAPTER EIGHT

Monsoon!

The very next day, the *Oriental* sailed right into a monster monsoon.

A monsoon is a seasonal wind that causes very heavy rains. The storm tossed the boat around on choppy waves. Many of the passengers became seasick and had to stay in their cabins.

Nellie Bly didn't quite get seasick this time. But the roughness of the waves made her feel faint.

Still, she found the monsoon exciting. She liked to watch the front of the ship rise up on a wave, then come crashing down.

She wrote: "The terrible swell of the sea during the monsoon was the most beautiful thing I ever saw. I would sit breathless on deck watching the bow of the ship standing upright on a wave, then dash headlong down as if intending to carry us to the bottom."

One night the monsoon was particularly strong and frightening. The enormous waves washed over the ship. Nellie Bly's cabin filled with water.

She tried to get away from the water. She crawled into her bunk.

Nellie Bly wondered if the ship would go down. But she wasn't thinking about whether or not she would die. She was more interested in whether she would complete her race.

If the ship went down, the brave reporter would never know if she could have made it around the world in seventy-five days. No one else would ever know, either.

Nellie Bly told herself that she should just stop worrying about it. If the ship sank, it sank. There was nothing she could do about it.

"If the ship does go down, there is time enough to worry when it's going," she wrote. "All the worry in the world cannot change it one way or another, and if the ship does not go down, I only waste so much time."

And so she went to sleep in her bunk.

The *Oriental* did not go down that night. Nor the next night. Nor the next. Nellie Bly did not have to worry about failing to finish her race. Not yet, anyway.

The weather continued to be rough. Once the ship

suddenly rolled to one side like a wagon that had fallen into a deep groove in the road. Nellie Bly was thrown out of her chair. She went flying clear across the deck.

Then another nasty wave sent the ship rolling to the other side. Nellie Bly grabbed an iron bar to keep herself from crashing through a skylight onto the deck below. It was a close call!

Despite the monsoon, Nellie Bly made it safe and sound to Hong Kong. In fact, the *Oriental* reached Hong Kong two whole days ahead of schedule.

At this point, Nellie Bly felt very confident. Everything was going well. She was sure to win her race against Phileas Fogg's record.

But Nellie Bly didn't know that Phileas Fogg was not her only competition. She had no idea that someone else was racing against *her!*

In Hong Kong, Nellie Bly went to the office of the Oriental and Occidental Steamship Company right away. It was the thirty-ninth day of her trip. She only had thirty-six more days to get to New York. But first, she had to make it to Japan.

"Will you tell me the date of the first sailing for Japan?" Nellie Bly asked a man at the Oriental and Occidental office.

"What is your name?" he asked her.

She told him. He looked at her nervously. He said, "You are going to be beaten."

"What?" Nellie Bly said. As far as she knew, she was right on schedule.

"You are going to lose it," the man insisted.

"What do you mean?" Nellie Bly demanded.

"Aren't you having a race around the world?" he asked her.

"Yes, quite right. I am running a race with Time," she replied.

The man shook his head. "Time? I don't think that's her name. The other woman…she is going to win. She left here three days ago."

Nellie Bly had a bad feeling in the pit of her stomach. This was the first time she had heard about another woman competing against her.

The man told Nellie Bly everything. Elizabeth Bisland was racing around the world in the opposite direction. Her editor at *Cosmopolitan* had offered the Oriental and Occidental Steamship Company a thousand or two thousand dollars to have the ship *Oceanic* leave San

Francisco two days ahead of time. And she had left Hong Kong three days ago.

Elizabeth Bisland was now way ahead of schedule, the man explained. And she, Nellie Bly, would be delayed in Hong Kong for five days. Elizabeth Bisland also had extra money to pay all the steamship companies so they would make their ships sail extra-fast for her.

At this rate, Elizabeth Bisland was sure to win. In fact, she intended to make the trip in *seventy* days. That was five days less than Nellie Bly's goal.

Nellie Bly listened to the man's story and tried to smile bravely. But she didn't feel like smiling. And she didn't feel brave.

Before she heard this news, she had no idea that she was racing against anything or anyone other than Phileas Fogg—and time itself. Her editors at *The World* had not even bothered to send her a cablegram about Elizabeth Bisland.

Now Nelly Bly had competition—*real* competition. And that person had every intention of making the trip in just seventy days!

CHAPTER NINE

An Unusual Christmas

Nellie Bly was not happy.

But back in New York, her editors at *The World* were *very* happy.

Nellie Bly's journey was making copies of *The World* newspaper sell like crazy. By the first of December, 268,230 copies were being sold each day. A week later, the number had reached 270,660. By December 16, the number was up to 273,090.

World readers were interested in whether or not Nellie Bly would beat Phileas Fogg's record. But now they were also interested in whether or not she would beat Elizabeth Bisland. With Elizabeth Bisland in the game, the race had gotten even more exciting.

The "Nellie Bly Guessing Match" was still a huge success. *The World* continued to receive thousands of entries with guesses about how many days, hours, minutes, and seconds it would take for Nellie Bly to get home to New York.

One person's entry was even written as a poem. It read:

Nellie Bly is flying high
On the China Sea;
With her goes the hope of one
Who wants to see Paree;
She'll get here in 74,
Sure as she's alive
Hours 12, minutes 10, and seconds 25.

Everyone in New York City—maybe even everyone in the country—seemed to be following Nellie Bly's journey. When would she make it home? *Would* she make it home? People talked about Nellie, read about Nellie, and held their breath.

Far away across the world, Nellie Bly was trying not to worry about Elizabeth Bisland. Whatever happens, will happen, she told herself.

Besides, it was almost Christmas. Nellie Bly had five whole days to wait in Hong Kong before the *Oceanic* set sail for Japan, then San Francisco. So she decided to spend Christmas in the city of Canton.

Canton is a city on the Pearl River of China. It lies about ninety miles northwest of Hong Kong.

A boat called the *Powan* took Nellie Bly to Canton. At the American Embassy there, she saw the American flag waving.

It filled her with happiness to see it. "That is the most beautiful flag in the world," she said.

Even though she missed America, Nellie Bly wanted to learn about the Chinese people. She called them "Celestials." Many years before Nellie Bly's time, China had been known as the "Celestial Empire," which means "heavenly empire." So for a while, many referred to the Chinese people as "Celestials."

Nellie Bly was curious about Canton. She took a tour of the city streets with other tourists from her boat. They were carried around in special chairs made out of willow branches. It took three Celestials to carry each chair.

During the tour, Nellie Bly admired the tiny shops with their wide-open doorways and carved signs. Every time she passed one of them, the Celestials rushed out to stare at her. They had no interest in the men in her group—just her. She wrote that they seemed to gaze at her as if she were "something new."

Nellie Bly didn't exactly spend a traditional Christmas in Canton. She didn't eat a fancy dinner or exchange presents with anyone or sing Christmas carols.

Instead, she asked to see the execution ground in Canton, where criminals guilty of certain crimes were put to death. As a reporter, Nellie Bly wanted to find out more about China than she could see from a tourist chair.

"Would you like to see some heads?" one of the guides asked Nellie Bly. He was talking about the heads of the criminals who had had their heads cut off.

Nellie Bly thought that he was lying about the heads just to impress her. She decided to challenge him.

"Certainly, bring on your heads!" she said.

She should have believed the guide. One of the men who worked for the guide walked over to a barrel filled with a whitish powder called lime. He reached in and pulled out a head!

But Nellie Bly didn't faint or scream. She just made notes so she could write about the story for *The World* and for everyone back home.

After the execution ground tour, Nellie Bly asked to

see a leper colony. There she saw many sick men, women, and children who suffered from a terrible skin disease called leprosy.

On Christmas Day, Nellie Bly found herself missing America very much. She thought about her family and friends back home, having a real Christmas dinner. She wished she could be there with them.

Instead the guide took Nellie Bly and the other tourists to a place called "Temple of the Dead." There they had their Christmas lunch.

It was probably the strangest way Nellie Bly would ever spend Christmas!

On December 28, Nellie Bly left Hong Kong on the *Oceanic*.

At that time, the *Oceanic* was one of the best ships that sailed the Pacific. It was fast, dependable, and comfortable. Nellie Bly knew that if any ship could get her to San Francisco on time, it was the *Oceanic*.

But first, the ship would be stopping in Yokohama, Japan.

Just before the ship reached Japan, Nellie Bly

celebrated New Year's Eve on board with her fellow passengers. It was so warm that Nellie Bly and the other women did not have to wear wraps. In the ship's dining hall, there was a special treat of oysters and champagne.

A Japanese man on the ship and his wife taught the other passengers a silly little song. They all sang it out loud:

> *Sweetly sings the donkey when he goes to grass,*
> *Sweetly sings the donkey when he goes to grass,*
> *Echo! Echo! Echo!*

The clock began to strike midnight. Nellie Bly and the others raised their glasses of champagne in the air. They sang the traditional New Year's song "Auld Lang Syne," which means "the good old times." Then they shook hands and wished each other a Happy New Year.

1889 was over. It was now 1890.

On the second day of the New Year, the *Oceanic* arrived in Yokohama. Nellie Bly fell in love with Japan. She wrote: "If I loved and married, I would say to my mate, 'Come, I know where Eden is,' and desert the land of my birth for Japan."

While she was in Japan, Nellie Bly saw small, pretty

houses made of wood and rice paper. She admired many beautiful gardens full of neat, perfect little trees and smooth stones arranged in patterns. She learned to eat rice and eel with chopsticks.

She also visited a special house where geisha girls sang and danced for audiences. The geisha girls wore silk kimonos and danced dainty dances. Nellie Bly was delighted with them. The geisha girls seemed delighted with her, too. They kept touching her bracelets and rings and hair and gloves. They asked her to come visit them again.

Nellie Bly also visited a famous temple called the Shiba temple. At the entrance, there was a gate with huge images of Japanese gods carved on it. Nellie Bly noticed that the gods were covered with chewed-up wads of paper.

Nellie Bly remarked that the schoolchildren in Japan must not be very well-behaved.

A man explained to her that the bits of paper had not been put there by mischievous children. The Japanese visitors, he told her, chewed paper and threw it at the gods. They believed that if the paper stuck, their wishes would come true.

At the temple, Nellie Bly saw an image of another god. This time, it was a statue. And the god had no nose!

It was explained to her that this had to do with another Japanese belief. The Japanese believed that rubbing the nose of the god would cure them of aches and pains. Nellie Bly realized that the Japanese people had rubbed the god's nose so often that it had completely disappeared!

All too soon, it was January 7—time to leave Japan. Nellie Bly was very sad to go. She had really enjoyed her time in that beautiful country.

But she was eager to get on with her journey, too. She had a record to break--and another "Miss B" to beat!

It was a bright, sunny morning when the *Oceanic* set sail for San Francisco, California. This part of the trip would take Nellie Bly all the way across the Pacific Ocean. As the ship left the harbor, a band started playing. It was the band from the *Omaha,* an American war ship that was docked in Yokohama.

The band played the songs "Home, Sweet Home," "Hail, Columbia," and "The Girl I Left Behind" in Nellie Bly's honor.

Nellie Bly waved her handkerchief until she could no longer see nor hear the band. She waved for so long that her arms were sore for days!

CHAPTER TEN

"For Nellie Bly We'll Win or Die"

To stay on schedule, Nellie Bly needed to reach San Francisco by January 20. That was only thirteen days away!

Luckily for her, the crew of the *Oceanic* was behind her one hundred percent. They had even written a little poem for her all over the ship's engines:

> *FOR NELLIE BLY*
> *WE'LL WIN OR DIE.*
> *JANUARY 20, 1890.*

Everything went smoothly until the third day of the crossing. Then the *Oceanic* ran into a bad storm at sea. The storm went on for twenty-four hours.

Nellie was beside herself with worry. The storm was sure to delay the ship. And such a delay could only mean one thing.

She was not going to finish her trip in time!

"If I fail," she said to the captain, "I will never return to New York. I would rather go in dead and successful than alive and behind time."

"Don't talk that way, my child," the captain said to her. "I would do anything for you in my power. I have worked the engines as they never were worked before. I have sworn at this storm until I have no words left. I have even prayed—I haven't prayed for years—but I prayed that this storm may pass over and that we may get you in on time."

Nellie Bly still had her pet monkey with her. For most of the journey since Singapore, she had kept the monkey in her cabin. The little animal had always been quiet and well-behaved.

But the storm seemed to frighten the monkey. He became nervous and excitable. At one point, he jumped on a woman's back and tried to bite her!

Nellie Bly realized that she would have to keep a closer eye on her pet. But she never suspected that her monkey might be in danger.

A rumor was going around the ship. People were terrified of the storm. Some of them began to whisper that there was a "Jonah" on board. A "Jonah" was someone who was thought to bring bad luck, like diseases or storms.

Someone on the *Oceanic* told Nellie Bly that many sailors believed that monkeys were Jonahs. As long as her monkey was on the ship, they said, the storm was sure to rage on and on.

They asked Nellie Bly if she would consider throwing her monkey overboard. That way, everyone told her, the ship's bad luck would end.

Nellie Bly didn't believe such nonsense. But she didn't know what to do to save her monkey. Then she found out that ministers were also believed to be Jonahs. The *Oceanic* had two ministers on board.

Nellie Bly calmly announced that if the ministers were thrown overboard, her monkey could be thrown overboard, too.

No one wanted to toss the poor ministers into the sea. They decided to ride out the storm. Nellie Bly's monkey was saved!

⧗

Finally, on January 20, Nellie Bly could see San Francisco from the deck of the *Oceanic*. She felt hopeful for the first time in many days.

But that hopefulness was not to last. Before the ship

reached port, a ship officer called the purser made a frantic announcement.

"The bill of health was left in Yokohama!" he cried out.

This did not sound good. Nellie Bly demanded to know what the purser was talking about.

The bill of health was a very important document saying that everyone on the ship was healthy and not carrying diseases from a foreign country.

The purser explained that no one would be permitted to get off the *Oceanic* until the next ship arrived from Japan with the bill of health. "That will be two weeks," he said miserably.

Nellie Bly couldn't bear to think about being stuck on the *Oceanic* for two whole weeks. "I would cut my throat, for I could not live and endure it," she told the purser in a cold, quiet voice.

Her threat encouraged him to search for the missing bill of health again. Fortunately, he found it. It was in the doctor's desk!

The next morning, Nellie Bly left the *Oceanic* carrying her monkey and her one small bag. The small bag was now stuffed full of souvenirs and presents from the new friends she had met on her trip.

And the monkey now had a name: McGinty!

Nellie Bly and McGinty finally set foot on American soil.

Nellie Bly had traveled more than 21,000 miles in just sixty-eight days. Now, all she had to do was get from San Francisco to New York in seven days.

Nellie Bly had 3,000 miles left in her journey.

She was safely back home in America. But would these last miles be the toughest yet?

CHAPTER ELEVEN

Three Thousand Miles to Go!

While Nellie Bly was aboard the *Oceanic*, *The World* had started sending its employees all over the country.

World reporters waited for Nelle Bly to arrive in Philadelphia, Pennsylvania; Ogden, Utah; and other American cities she would be traveling through. They planned to welcome her home, escort her to the next city, and send reports about her progress back to New York City.

But then Mother Nature struck again. A winter snowstorm blasted the Central Pacific region with snowflakes the size of crackers. It was the worst storm in the area in over ten years.

In fact, a group of people who were supposed to meet Nellie Bly in San Francisco never made it there. They were stuck in the Sierra Nevada Mountains of

California for over fifty hours. Their train couldn't pass through the storm.

The storm forced *The World* to make a big decison. The train tracks were not likely to be cleared for at least a week. At that rate, Nellie Bly would never make it back to New York on time.

There was only one hope. The newspaper paid for a special train to bring Nellie Bly home. The train would take different tracks that had not been affected by the storm. The tracks ran southeast from San Francisco and then north toward Chicago rather than directly east through the storm. That way, Nellie Bly would have a fighting chance to finish on time.

But would she do it?

There was no time to waste worrying. Nellie Bly and McGinty got on board the special train headed toward Chicago. In Chicago they would switch to another train bound for New York.

"What time do you want to reach New York, Miss Bly?" the general passenger agent of the train company asked her.

"No later than Saturday evening," Nellie Bly replied. But she didn't think there was any way the train could make it that quickly.

"Very well," the man promised her. "We will put you there on time." Nellie Bly believed him.

The rest of the trip was a crazy, thrilling whirlwind. Nellie Bly felt as though she were flying across the continent. Cheering fans turned out at every stop. In one town, a band played "My Nellie's Blue Eyes" for her. In another town, by Nellie Bly's account, 10,000 people showed up to greet her. The mayor of one city presented her with a certificate on behalf of all the citizens.

"Americans turned out to do honor to an American girl who had been the first to make a record of a flying trip around the world," Nellie Bly wrote. "And I rejoiced with them that it was an American girl who had done it."

On board the train, Nellie Bly received flowers and cablegrams. The telegrams were addressed simply to "Nellie Bly, Nellie Bly's Train." By now Nellie Bly was the most famous woman in America. She didn't need a real address. Every cable office knew where to send her messages!

In Chicago, Nellie Bly switched from the special train

to a regular train. Compared to the super-fast special train from San Francisco, the regular train seemed to creep along the tracks.

Then Nellie Bly received a cablegram that had missed her in San Francisco. It was from Monsieur and Madame Verne back in France. It read:

Mr. Verne wishes the following message to be handed to Nellie Bly the moment she touches American soil: "Monsieur and Madame Jules Verne address their sincerest felicitations to Miss Nellie Bly at the moment when that intrepid young lady sets foot on the soil of America."

The cablegram made Nellie Bly very happy. She held onto it tightly as the train made its way east.

The train stopped in Logansport, Indiana; Columbus, Ohio; and Harrisburg, Pennsylvania. In Harrisburg, a group of Philadelphia newspaper reporters got onto the train to escort Nellie Bly to her final destination.

Nellie Bly finally reached Jersey City, which is just across the river from New York City. It was the last stop on the train—and the last stop of her long, long journey.

An enormous crowd was waiting for Nellie Bly. Everyone was shouting and cheering. Cannons boomed.

Nellie Bly took a deep breath and stepped onto the platform. She took off her cap to cheer with the crowd.

But she wasn't cheering just because she had traveled around the world in 72 days, 6 hours, 11 minutes, and 14 seconds—8 days ahead of Phileas Fogg's record. She was cheering because she was so glad to be back home again.

The mayor of Jersey City tried to give a speech. It was hard for him to be heard above the cannons and the screaming crowd.

"The American girl can no longer be misunderstood!" the mayor shouted. "She will be recognized as determined, independent, able to take of herself wherever she may go."

Once again, Nellie Bly had proved that the impossible could be done!

CHAPTER TWELVE

"The Best Reporter in America"

Nellie Bly broke Phileas Fogg's record by eight days. She even finished the trip three days ahead of her own goal—and beat Elizabeth Bisland by several more days. Elizabeth Bisland had missed several connections in Europe and had many other problems on her trip.

Nellie Bly was a heroine at home and around the world. But after she returned to New York she felt that her employers at *The World* didn't appreciate what she had done. She was angry that they didn't offer to pay her more money after she made the record-breaking trip. They didn't even say "thank you" to her.

And so she quit her job at *The World*.

But Nellie Bly didn't quit working. Later in 1890, she wrote and published an autobiography called *Nellie Bly's Book*. It became a best-seller. She also wrote short stories for magazines. And she went all over the country giving lectures about her experiences.

All of these things helped Nellie Bly make money. One year she made $25,000. That was a lot of money in the 1890s.

Nellie Bly had said that she would never return to *The World*. But in 1893, she changed her mind. A new editor had taken over the paper. He made her a good job offer. So by September of that year, Nellie was writing articles again. The articles were as smart and brave and interesting as ever.

In 1895 Nellie Bly met a gentleman on a train. His name was Robert Seaman. He was an iron manufacturer.

Nellie Bly and Robert Seaman got married just a few days after they met. He was seventy-two. She was thirty.

Nellie Bly decided to stop being a reporter. She wanted to spend all her time being with her new husband and throwing parties for their friends.

But Robert Seaman died in 1904. After his death, Nellie Bly began to run his company. She turned out to be really good at the job. The company started to make more money. Nellie Bly was able to pay the workers better salaries and make sure their workplace was safe. That was very important to her.

But everything changed in 1912. Nellie Bly discovered that some of the workers had been stealing money from her company. She had to go to court, which cost her more money. Finally, all her money ran out and she lost the company.

In summer of 1914, Nellie Bly went to Austria. She needed a vacation to recover from losing her company.

While she was in Austria, World War I broke out. Nellie Bly's vacation was over. But a new stage in her career as a reporter was just beginning.

She started writing articles about the war for the *New York Evening Journal.* When she returned to the U.S. in 1919, she kept writing for the paper. She had always enjoyed being a reporter.

Nellie Bly didn't have a big comeback. By that time she was fifty-five years old. And no one even seemed to remember who she was!

But Nellie Bly wasn't discouraged. Just as she had in earlier years, she wrote many powerful articles. She often wrote about "underdogs," people who weren't seen as being as strong, successful, or lucky.

Nellie Bly didn't just write about people who were less fortunate. She searched through the streets of the city for homeless children. Then she tried to find homes for them. She wanted to help people in need wherever she went and whenever she could.

In 1922 Nellie Bly died of pneumonia. Many newspapers wrote stories about her life. They told of everything she had done for women through her work. Nellie Bly would always be remembered because she had made it easier for women to become reporters. She had been brave and tough enough to do the job when there were very few other women reporters.

The *Pittsburgh Dispatch* said: "She was the best reporter in America."

Nellie Bly would have been very proud.

Bibliography

Kroeger, Brooke. *Nellie Bly: Daredevil, Reporter, Feminist.* Times Books, 1994.

Marks, Jason. *Around The World in 72 Days: The Race Between Pulitzer's Nellie Bly and Cosmopolitan's Elizabeth Bisland.* Gemittarius Press, 1993.

Peck, Ira, ed. *Nellie Bly's Book: Around The World in 72 Days.* Twenty-First Century Books, 1998.

Verne, Jules. William Butcher, trans. *Around The World in Eighty Days.* Oxford University Press, 1995.

Emma Dodge Hanson

About the Author

Nancy Butcher is the *New York Times* best-selling author of many books for children, including titles in the *Two of a Kind*, *Wishbone*, and *Ghostwriter Mysteries* series. She is also the co-author of the *Fire-us* trilogy for teens: *The Kindling*, *The Keepers of the Flame*, and *The Kiln*. Born in Japan, she now lives with her family in New York City and Saratoga Springs, NY.

MORE ABOUT THE
NELLIE BLY
STORY

How Nellie Bly Got Her Name

Nellie Bly did not start out her life as Nellie Bly.

She was born on May 5, 1864 in Cochran Mills, Pennsylvania as Elizabeth Jane Cochran. When she was a little girl, everyone called her "Pink." This may be because her mother often had her wear frilly pink dresses.

When Pink was fifteen, she decided to attend the Indiana State Normal School in Indiana, Pennsylvania. A "normal school" was a private school that

Nellie Bly in her traveling outfit

Nellie Bly

trained young women and men for teaching and business jobs. At school, Pink signed her name "Elizabeth Jane Cochrane." No one knows for sure why she added the extra "e" to her last name. She was still called Pink by her friends and family.

When Pink was twenty, she got her first job as a reporter, at the *Pittsburgh Dispatch.* Her starting pay would be five dollars a week. The managing editor, George Madden, wanted a special byline for her. A "byline" is the name a reporter uses for his or her stories. It was not proper for the few women reporters of that time to use their real names for bylines.

George Madden asked the writers and editors at the *Dispatch* for suggestions. What should they call their new reporter? One of them suggested "Nelly Bly." Nelly Bly was the name of a popular song by Stephen Foster, the composer of "Oh, Susannah" and other famous songs. George Madden was in a big hurry for a new byline for his new reporter. He decided

Nellie Bly

THE "NELLIE BLY"
caps for young ladies

Many young women wanted to be like Nellie Bly.

that "Nelly Bly" was just fine. But maybe the editor was in *too* much of a hurry. He got the spelling of "Nelly" wrong and changed it to "Nell*ie*"!

So Elizabeth Jane Pink Cochrane became forever known as Nellie Bly.

Around the World in…79 Days?

Nellie Bly set out to beat the record of book hero Phileas Fogg, who circled the globe in eighty days.

Or was it seventy-nine?

Phileas Fogg was the main character in Jules Vernes' novel *Around the World in 80 Days*. In the story, Phileas Fogg was an English gentleman who lived in Victorian London.

On the evening of October 2, 1872, he found himself making a crazy bet. He bragged to his friends at the Reform Club—a "gentle-men's club" where men ate meals, played cards, and had conversations with each other—that he could travel around the

The characters Phileas Fogg and Passepartout from the movie *Around the World in 80 Days* world in eighty days. No one had ever dared to do such a thing before.

Phileas Fogg bet 20,000 pounds, which was half of his fortune. He promised that he would be back at the Reform Club by 8:45 p.m. on December 21. If he wasn't back by then, he would lose the bet—and the 20,000 pounds.

Phileas Fogg went home and told his servant Passepartout to get ready for a trip around the world. They had ten minutes to pack. Passepartout did as he was told, and the two men hurried to the train station. They got on the 8:45 train bound for the boat to Calais, France.

Their journey was full of adventure and excitement. The two men traveled by train, steamship, carriage, yacht, sled, and even elephant!

In India, Phileas Fogg met a beautiful widow named Aouda. Aouda joined Phileas Fogg and Passepartout on their travels. In Hong Kong, Passepartout got lost. Luckily, he found his way back to his master and Aouda. But in America, Passepartout was attacked and carried off by Indians. Phileas Fogg managed to rescue him.

When Phileas Fogg, Passepartout, and Aouda finally reached London, it looked as if Phileas Fogg would be five minutes late. Phileas Fogg couldn't stand

the thought of losing his bet. But Aouda cheered him up and saved the day. She asked Phileas Fogg to marry her. She also convinced him not to give up. He decided to go through with the bet, even if he was too late to win.

Phileas Fogg marched into the Reform Club with his head held high. Everyone in the club was shocked and amazed. It turned out that Phileas Fogg had won his bet, after all. He hadn't made the trip in eighty days. He had finished it in *seventy-nine* days!

Phileas Fogg *lost* a day off his trip because he traveled east around the world instead of west. He hadn't realized that all the different time zones and time changes would

The Taj Mahal,
Agra, India

help him save time and win the bet.

In real life, Nellie Bly skipped India in order to save time. If Phileas Fogg had not stopped in India, he would have saved time, too. That was what his servant Passepartout pointed out to him in the end. They could have made the trip in *seventy-eight* days!

'ROUND THE WORLD OR BUST!

What Happened to Elizabeth Bisland?

Elizabeth Bisland may have lost her race against Nellie Bly. But she did beat Phileas Fogg's record by four days. Of course, it was Nellie Bly who got all the glory. After all, she beat both Phileas Fogg *and* Elizabeth Bisland!

Elizabeth Bisland didn't have parades thrown in her honor like Nellie Bly. But she did go on to lead a successful and

Elizabeth Bisland

Photo courtesy of Lafcadio Hearn Collection, Howard-Tilton Memorial Library, Tulane University

interesting life. She wrote a series of seven articles about her trip for *Cosmopolitan* magazine. In 1891, the articles were published as a book called *In Seven Stages: A Flying Trip Around the World.*

That same year, Elizabeth Bisland married a well-known New York lawyer named Charles Wetmore. The couple later moved to Washington, D.C. There Elizabeth Bisland Wetmore joined the Women's Democratic Club. She also published several more books.

After her husband died in 1919, Elizabeth Bisland Wetmore moved to a big plantation in Charlottesville, Virginia. During World War I, she went to London, England to help take care of sick and wounded patients in an army hospital. After the war was over, she returned to the United States and became president of a medical clinic. The clinic took care of young working women who didn't have very much money.

A World War I nurse

Elizabeth Bisland Wetmore died of pneumonia at the age of sixty-seven. One newspaper remembered her as "the Bessie Bisland who raced against Time and Nellie Bly around the world."

Nellie Bly Travels the World
Again...on a Stamp!

In 2002 the U.S. Postal Service gave Nellie Bly her very own stamp. Three other women reporters throughout American history also received this honor. They were Marguerite Higgins, Ethel L. Payne, and Ida M. Tarbell. The stamps were part of a special "Women in Journalism" series. Nellie Bly was chosen because of her outstanding work and dedication. She was also honored because she helped pave the way for future women reporters.

Designer and artist for the United States Postal Service's *Women in Journalism* commemorative stamps series: Fred Otnes